THE TRIUMPH JOURNEY

Melanie Davis & Jana Nielsen

All materials presented are for educational and support purposes. The authors make no claim on the implied or expressed therapeutic value of *The TRIUMPH Journey*. Any person having difficulty in handling their traumas is encouraged to seek professional counseling services.

CONTENTS

How to Use this Book ········· 5

Introduction: *Write and LIVE Your Triumph Story* ········· 7

Section One: *Character Development* ········· 17

Section Two: *The Role of Conflict in Your Triumph Story* ········· 35

Section Three: *Paradigm Shift* ········· 45

Section Four: *Circle of Control* ········· 59

Section Five: *Believing You Can Achieve* ········· 63

Section Six: *Supporting Characters* ········· 71

Section Seven: *Finding Your Mission* ········· 81

Section Eight: *Charting Your Course* ········· 87

Section Nine: *Character Arcs* ········· 97

Section Ten: *Envisioning Your TRIUMPHANT Future* ········· 107

Appendix: ········· 117

    Seven Rules of Exceptional Writing ········· 119

    Additional Worksheets ········· 125

    Additional Writing Pages ········· 139

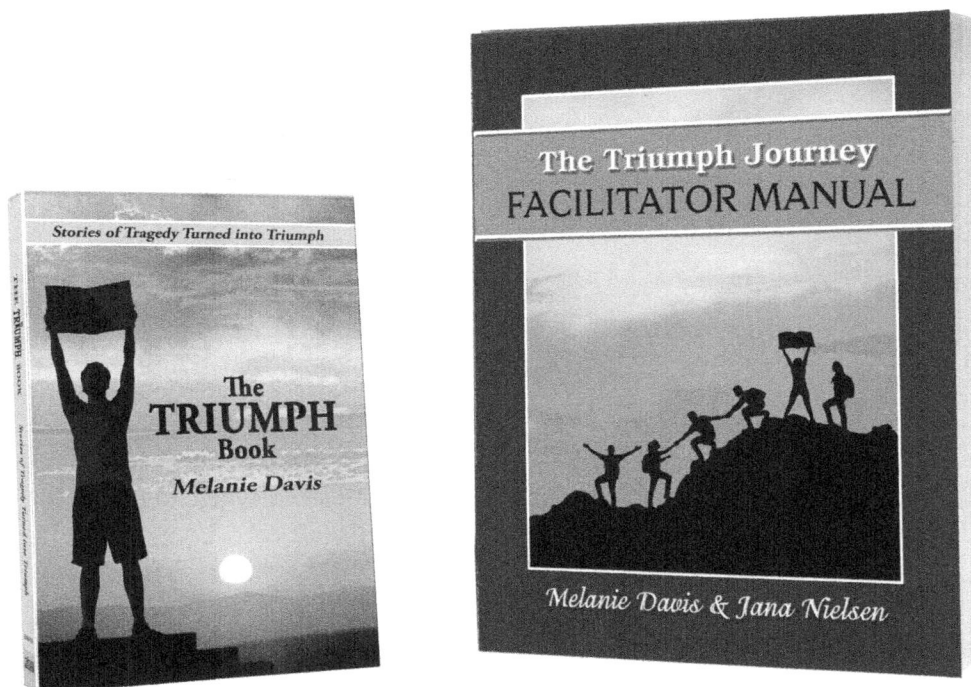

How to Use The Triumph Journey Workbook

The Triumph Journey workbook leads participants through several evidence-based practices such as narrative therapy, logotherapy, recognizing personal strengths and resilience, group sharing, meditation, gratitude journaling, art therapy, goal setting and visualization.

In *The Triumph Journey* participants use story-writing elements to empower them through life's challenges. In their personal Triumph Journey, participants learn to see themselves as heroes, use conflicts as stepping stones, experience paradigm shifts, plan and implement personalized pathways to success, recognize opportunities in their difficulties, and maintain an optimistic approach to life.

The Triumph Journey is most effectively used in a group setting with no more than four group members per facilitator. Each participant should have their own copy of *The Triumph Journey* workbook. Facilitators are encouraged to use *The Triumph Journey Facilitator Manual. Section Five* uses stories from *The Triumph Book* by Melanie Davis which can be downloaded as a free eBook from *www.TriumphPress.com* by filling in a form at the bottom of the home page. from the bottom of the **Triumph Press** home page or order a print copy on Amazon (be sure to include the author's name when searching for it).

INTRODUCTION

Write & Live Your Triumph Story

"What role do you want to play in your life: the victim, survivor, or hero?" - Wendy Watson Nelson

Life is a gift. It is the greatest gift any of us have, and in some ways, it is our only *true possession*! Everything you own, every person you know, every place you go, every experience you have can be lost or come to an end. It is said that the only guarantee in life is change, but as long as you are breathing and walking on this earth, *one thing that doesn't change* is that you are **ALIVE!**

Life is an **EPIC JOURNEY!** It is a story you are creating every day you live and with each decision you make. While there will always be things that are out of your control, developing your life into a story that is filled with success, happiness, and TRIUMPH is completely up to you. You can **DECIDE** to be the hero of your own story.

"The only person you are destined to become is the person you decide to be."
- Ralph Waldo Emerson

This **Triumph Journey** workbook will assist you to *Discover, Write and LIVE* your **TRIUMPH STORY**! It will assist you to conquer the adversities you face, achieve the dreams you envision, and to make a difference in the world...because that's what heroes do! They are respected, appreciated, remembered, and emulated; heroes live adventures that matter. *You can be a hero!* No matter what is going on in your life, regardless of the seeming setbacks, poverty, loneliness, abuse, or difficulties you may be facing right now, from this moment forward, decide to be a hero. Write your Triumph Story and you will not fail. That message is so important, it deserves repeating: **DECIDE** *to be a hero, AND YOU WILL NOT FAIL!*

Heroes are not perfect. They aren't free of mistakes, trouble, hardship, or even regret. *Heroes may even have a criminal record!* What makes someone a hero is the wisdom gained and implemented in his or her life, the purpose discovered, the quest boldly sought after, and the resiliency developed as they overcome the obstacles that stand between them and their destiny.

Triumph doesn't just happen; you have to step up and *BE* the hero of your own story. Becoming the hero is something you decide and work towards; it is how you choose to identify yourself. The sections of this workbook will provide the process, direction, and tools needed to determine how you want your life story to unfold.

"It is not the mountain we conquer but ourselves." - Edmond Hillary

Additionally, this program is an actual story writing course. In this workbook, you will learn many of the core elements in storytelling and how to use them to become the author of your life, especially the chapters that are yet ahead for you to experience.

Meet the Authors:

Melanie Davis
Triumph Press Founder

After suffering the loss of my seven-month daughter, Brynn, to Sudden Infant Death Syndrome (SIDS), I found healing and purpose by writing and then sharing my story with those who could be encouraged and inspired by the wisdom and purpose I found in her death.

From this experience, I went on to become the founder of **Triumph Press** which publishes *The Triumph Book Series* as well as the books and stories of others who have overcome great adversities.

In addition to publishing people's books, I developed a narrative therapy/peer-to-peer mentoring process of recording and sharing *Triumph Stories* using a workbook called **The Triumph Program**. It covers many types of grief and loss, including bereavement and a special edition to assist veterans with PTSD.

The workbook you are holding, **The Triumph Journey,** is inspired by all of the work I have done helping people to heal by processing their life experiences in writing. This version of the program is unique as it teaches the elements of storytelling and uses them to write both a Triumphant and *HEROIC* plan for your life that will become your true story as you Develop and Live it on purpose!

I invited one of my dear, life-long friends, Jana Nielsen, to contribute by sharing her stories as they relate to the topics in each section of this workbook. As you will learn, she has faced and overcome some of life's most challenging difficulties including mental health issues since childhood, abuse and domestic violence, drug addiction, institutionalization, and becoming homeless for a period of time. Jana has exceptional wisdom to share and reading her examples can help the principles I teach become more applicable.

You will have the opportunity to discover more of my story as you read **The Triumph Book** which is a companion to this program used in *Section Five*. Mine is the first story in that book.

Next, I have asked Jana to introduce herself and prepare you for the JOURNEY to come:

Jana Nielsen
JanOvation Founder

I am an artist, illustrator, graphic designer, and writer. I am also trained as a peer counselor. My top five strengths are empathy, being loving, creative, full of ideas, and goal oriented. Later in this book, you will find your own top strengths.

If you saw my home, you'd notice it is somewhat decorated in Christmas colors and themes. I love to give homemade items, so you might say that it's perpetually Christmas at my house.

I've had many joys in my journey of life. Even the memory of these has kept me going when times have gotten tough. But the times I've learned and grown as a person the most were through periods of difficulty. Each one was very much a struggle for me, but when I've broken through to the wisdom and empathy on the other side, I've been able to help others.

Melanie asked that I share some of my story here and throughout the book. I hope to tell you of the strength and lessons I have learned through those trials. Maybe something I've written from my experience will resonate with you.

Cheer Up

I grew up with untreated bipolar disorder and had severe depression at the early age of eight. This lasted until I was finally treated with the correct set of medications that worked for me which didn't happen until well into adulthood.

I remember as a child asking a man who was my neighbor, "What is depression?"

He told me, "Well it's when an adult is really sad and can't find happiness again."

I thought, "Hmm...If I were an adult, I would say I have depression."

In the 1970s, I don't think many people knew about childhood depression. My parents did all they could for me with the limited knowledge that they had at the time. Back then they didn't really know about chemical imbalances. Everyone just tried to push through it and cheer up!

No matter how hard I tried, I couldn't just cheer up.

You'll see how I finally worked through it later in this workbook.

Seeking Refuge from the Storm

When my first husband and I moved to Springfield Oregon and had two beautiful girls, one age five and the other fourteen months old, I found out he was abusing them. I confronted him about it and he confirmed my suspicions. Within a week I packed the few items that would fit into a suitcase I purchased from Goodwill and we left.

We had nowhere to go, so I knocked on a friend's door. He took us in for a while and was very kind.

After about a month and a half, this friend persuaded my parents (who lived across the country) to take us in. The night before we were to fly out, my lawyer called and told me that my husband was going to meet me at the plane and serve me with kidnapping papers. So, we got an early flight out by standby that night. All we owned, fit into that one suitcase and I had a $50 bill that my friend gave us for food at the airports along the way.

There was a long road of healing ahead.

The Battle

When we got to Florida, I stayed with my parents for a while. I couldn't work because of my bipolar disorder and chronic fatigue.

My oldest daughter, though only age five, went through intense counseling for the abuse by her father. The abuse was so severe that the counseling center sent its own lawyer to represent her in court.

The custody battle went on for two years with many lawyers dumping my ex when they found out what he did, and with him trying to make it seem that I was an unfit mother because of my bipolar disorder.

This was a dark time for me. I loved being with my girls, but I was undergoing some severe depression.

Just before the divorce and custody hearing, when my ex husband saw that my oldest daughter had her own lawyer, he signed a custody agreement with my specifications.

When we got into court for the lawyers to present these papers, the judge said something to the effect of, "Why isn't this in criminal court?" He told my ex that if he ever stopped paying his child support, he would really crack down on him.

He never did one thing on the custody agreement to be able to see the girls. That was fine by me. I wouldn't let him have any contact with them until he did. One thing I can say for him is that he always paid his child support.

Because of this experience, I gained empathy and learned some coping mechanisms to get through hard times. You will learn these later in the book.

Fairwood Days

Our time in Fairwood, Washington was one of my most joyful. The girls and I enjoyed walks together. We had fun making crafts. Even chores were done as a family team.

I read to them at night from a collection of children's books that they would choose every night. I would cry when I read, *I'll Love You Forever* by Robert Munch. In that book, a mother sings a song to her sleeping child. Somehow, I had an impression that I would not be able to be there for my girls' entire childhoods. So, I would sneak into their room at night and softly sing to their sleeping forms, the song from the book, *I'll Love You Forever*, and I would cry.

I learned to love with all my heart unconditionally. And to enjoy the precious little moments I had with my girls.

Fatigue

As time went on, the chronic fatigue got worse and worse. I also started having severe migraines that kept me in bed all the time. They were so bad that all I could do for dinner was crawl to the living room and teach the girls how to make macaroni and cheese from the couch as the kitchen was next to it. They were ages eight and twelve. I felt like I was neglecting them. I loved my girls so much and was afraid I would have to give them up to keep them from being neglected!

I couldn't get as much help as I needed from family and I had few resources at the time. I thought, *if I get married to someone, maybe he can help with their physical needs and I could assist with their emotional ones.*

I married the first guy to come along. Little did I know how devastating this would be to our small family.

As a single mom, I had yet to learn to ask for all the help I needed and to keep asking until I got it. I have learned that now and that settling is never a good option.

Evil is Real!

The guy I married is named Chris. Up till I married him, I thought that nobody chooses to be evil, they just don't know how to love and be good yet. I was wrong.

He introduced me to meth shortly after we were married. That was the start of a long road down the addiction path for me.

Domestic abuse started shortly after that. His main objective was to take all our money: my SSI and the kids' child support. He isolated us from my family by cutting off the long-distance on our phone. (My family and good friends were all long-distance.)

Unknown to me, he was drugging and poisoning my food and drinks so he could take all our money when it came in and to stop me from protecting my kids. I know he was drugging and poisoning me because after I left, a friend of his stopped by and told me he (the friend) had sold Chris some heavy sedatives. Chris told him that they were for me and that I liked them crushed up in my Squirt! How could this friend know that my favorite soft drink was Squirt?!

Unlike the way Chris described me, I hated anything that would make me tired. I used meth to be able to stay awake for my kids, although it never worked very well.

Chris's drugging me made me fall asleep, even while eating, and sometimes for days. At first, I thought it was my Chronic fatigue getting worse. But later I suspected he was making me sick. When I told him that I thought he was drugging and poisoning me, he said I was crazy and challenged me to prove it. Finally, when we went to stay at a shelter, my kids said they saw him put stuff in my food and drinks.

Four months after we split up, Chris called saying he wanted to get back together. I told him I knew about the drugging and poisoning. He said, "You can't blame that on me; you were getting on my nerves!" And there it was; he had admitted it to me on the phone.

I learned that evil is real and to protect myself by choosing whom I associate with wisely. This was an important lesson for me to learn! Later in the book, you will experience an activity to help you with choosing and keeping good friends.

Without Them

After Chris stole all our money, we were evicted. He went back to live with his mom while we couldn't find any shelters that were open. The kids and I were about to be homeless. I didn't want that for them, so I farmed them out to family members to keep them from having to live the unforgiving life of the streets. I couldn't get anyone to take both girls, so they went to different families in different states.

I was sure my brother and sister-in-law would treat my youngest daughter well, but my oldest daughter went to someone on her dad's side of the family. I wasn't sure if she would be okay there, but they took me to court for temporary custody and won, so I didn't have a choice in the matter.

It was such a struggle not to be able to care for my children while I was homeless. I love them so much and wanted the best for them, but since they were with other people, things happened, and it didn't work out the way I thought it should. Such was the case with my oldest daughter. I saw those who were taking care of her, not treating her how I would and I was distraught about it. I wanted to snag both my daughters back, but I had no home for them to go to.

Meditating on the situation brought me to a new perspective. I realized that I had to let go.

From this experience, I learned to let go of the things I had no control over. This was a difficult lesson for me because all I ever wanted in life was to be a good mom to my kids! Now, I had to let go of this. It was a hard thing to put in someone else's basket.

In this workbook, you will find an activity that helped me learn to let go of what I can't control.

On my first day homeless, I only had a small backpack with a few things. The rest of my belongings were put into storage where I couldn't get to it on foot; it was far away and I had no car.

I started by going to the store because I didn't know where else to go. There, I ran into someone I knew who said I could stay with her and her husband for one night.

I spent most of my time couch surfing. The main place I stayed was David's home. He lived in senior housing and wasn't supposed to have anyone live with him, so I snuck in and out. I was homeless for two years.

Later in this book, you will learn how I found meaning in life at that time.

So Much Pain

Even after I was able to rent an apartment, I struggled with debilitating migraines. In fact they've been my nemesis most of my adult life. I had gotten on a medication for a while, to ease the pain, that really helped, but it also made me put on a lot of weight. Once I reached 300 pounds, I said goodbye to that medication.

The migraines came back as soon as the medication was out of my system. A few years ago, the migraines ramped up until I was pretty much bedridden. I could only get out of bed to go to the bathroom and grab a quick drink of water, or some microwavable prepackaged food. Then, back to my quiet dark room and to bed I went.

It would be two years of this before I was able to get any better. I still have the migraines, just not as frequent or long-lasting as they were back then.

Today

When Melanie asked me to write this book with her, I felt she was inspired. I want to share the coping mechanisms that helped me get through these troubling times. I desire to lift others and help them do and become more in life. Most of all, I want to help others see themselves as the bright shining stars and heroes that they are by learning to victoriously face the hills and mountains of their journey and keep climbing!

I hope to share some light, experience, and coping skills that have helped me in my journey. Maybe some of what I write will give you strength and courage for the road you have ahead of you. As unpredictable as it may seem, you do have a TRIUMPHANT FUTURE!

Special Note:

Going forward you will be able to identify my contributions to this workbook in the light grey shaded boxes like this one.

SECTION ONE
Character Development

"Knowing yourself is the beginning of all wisdom." –Aristotle

Every good story centers around a **Main Character**, often referred to as "the protagonist." This term can also be interchanged with the word "hero." The Main Character is the person in a story who readers are most interested in and feel the greatest compassion towards. As you begin to write your life story, it is critical that you come to know the Main Character. *How well do you know yourself?*

Seeing yourself as the protagonist or the hero of your adventure results in greater **Self-Respect**. Having confidence in and loving oneself, is the *FOUNDATIONAL TRAIT* of a successful life. Self-Respect is not having a blown-up ego; it involves taking responsibility for who you are and where you are going. The importance of Self-Respect cannot be overstated because it determines all the decisions you make; how you treat yourself, and the way you allow others to treat you.

"Never dull your shine for somebody else."
- Tyra Banks

A healthy level of Self-Respect gives you the confidence to set firm boundaries and helps you recognize your values, strengths, and weaknesses. Self-Respect is an essential trait of a hero; it is actually an INNER POWER that has to be intentionally developed. It comes from life experiences, facing and overcoming obstacles, and **knowing yourself**!

Hanalei Vierra, Ph.D., author of the book, *The True Heart of a Man*, defines Self-Respect as "a form of self-love wherein a person values his or her own unique and unrepeatable approach to living life. It is having an understanding and appreciation of the underlying character traits of one's true self....."

It took me a long time to start to respect myself. All through my childhood and early adulthood, I longed for someone to respect me. I didn't realize that I was the one who had to do it first. In fact, even as a small child, I hated myself! I thought I was so imperfect that dying would be an option to free those I loved from the burden of me.

It was well into my adulthood when I heard these words, *"Failure is part of growth; you can get back up."* That was an epiphany for me!

I slowly learned to treat myself kindly, especially in self-talk. I began to speak to myself as if I were a precious loved one. I told myself that I was okay even if I wasn't perfect, that I had innate value, and that I was uniquely needed in the world. It wasn't easy. I sometimes caught myself listening to that ugly, mean voice that kept telling me lies like it did in my childhood. Eventually, I learned to counter those lies with beautiful truths about myself: that I am lovable, that I am creative, that I matter!

Now I know who I am. I like myself now. I recognize my strengths and use my weaknesses to improve myself. I can honestly say that. It's amazing!

"When there is no enemy within, the enemies outside cannot hurt you"
- African Proverb

"Pay no attention to what the critics say.
A statue has never been erected in honor of a critic."
- Jean Sibelius

The process of Writing, Discovering, and *LIVING* your Triumph Story begins with **Character Development**. It is getting to know the Main Character (you), by illustrating his or her qualities, interests, personality traits, tragedies, and triumphs. So, how well do you know yourself? The answer might surprise you... **Section One** is the space where you introduce your authentic self *to yourself*, to those in your Triumph Group, and to people in the future who will come to know the hero that is being further developed in this program.

You will learn much more about yourself as you go through each of the sections in this workbook, but answering the following questions will "set the stage" for the discovery and growth that is coming.

"If you could catch a glimpse of your true worth,
with all your strengths and potential,
you would rise up and never be the same again."
-Jana Nielsen

Let's try to catch that Glimpse...

Some **Definitions** to help with the **Strengths Inventory**

- **Articulate** - expressing oneself readily, clearly, and effectively
- **Charismatic** - exercising a compelling charm that inspires devotion in others
- **Charitable** - full of love for and goodwill toward others
- **Bold** - showing or a fearless daring spirit
- **Critical Thinker** - exercising or involving careful judgment or judicious evaluation
- **Diligent** - characterized by steady, earnest, and energetic effort : painstaking
- **Dynamic** - marked by usually continuous and productive activity or change
- **Empathetic** - the action of understanding, being aware of, being sensitive to, and vicariously experiencing the feelings, thoughts, and experience of another
- **Entrepreneurial** - having to do with the creation and development of economic ventures
- **Flexible** - characterized by a ready capability to adapt to new, different, or changing requirements or able to bend the body well
- **Gracious** - marked by kindness and courtesy, tact and delicacy
- **Humble** - to act honorably, and be teachable, not haughty
- **Ingenuity** - someone's ability to think of smart new ways of doing something
- **Integrity** - the quality of being honest and having strong moral principles that you refuse to change
- **Mentor** - a trusted counselor or guide
- **Modest** - neither bold nor self-assertive and placing an honest estimate on one's abilities or worth or observing the proprieties of decent dress and behavior
- **Persistence** - the ability to keep doing something difficult
- **Resilient** - able to be happy, successful, etc. again after something difficult or bad has happened
- **Self-Aware** - knowing and understanding yourself very well
- **Strategic** - able to achieve a plan with several variables involved
- **Teachable** - able and willing to be taught and learn new things
- **Virtuous** - having good moral qualities and behavior
- **Vigilant** - always being careful to notice things, especially possible danger

20

Strengths Inventory

Adventurous	Full of ideas	Persuasive
Ambitious	Generous	Persistence
Articulate	Gentle	Powerful
Beautiful	Goal-oriented	Prepared
Bold	Good friend	Productive
Brave	Good judgment	Professional
Calm	Good listener	Prompt
Charismatic	Good negotiator	Purposeful
Charitable	Gracious	Resilient
Cheerful	Happy	Respectful
Clever	Hard-working	Responsible
Compassionate	Helpful	Self-Aware
Confident	Honest	Self-Confidence
Courageous	Humble	Self-Control
Creative	Ingenuity	Sense of Humor
Critical Thinker	Integrity	Skilled
Curious	Inventive	Spiritual
Daring	Kind	Story-Teller
Dependable	Knowledgeable	Strategic
Determined	Leader	Strong work ethic
Diligent	Logical	Survivor
Dynamic	Loving	Talented
Easygoing	Loyal	Teachable
Empathetic	Mentor	Troubleshooter
Endurance	Modest	Trusting
Energetic	Open-Minded	Unique
Entrepreneurial	Optimistic	Unselfish
Enthusiastic	Organized	Virtuous
Faithful	Outgoing	Vigilant
Fearless	Passionate	Well-rounded
Flexible	Patient	Wise
Forgiving	Peacemaker	Sense of Wonder

Character Development Questions

Use the following questions to write about your Journey and experiences that have molded you into who you are today.

1. **Who are you? (Character Development)**
   What interests, skills, history, background, and other information can you share that will help readers identify with and know you better?

2. What difficulties did you face growing up?

- What struggles did you experience at home? (Single parent, alcohol/drugs abuse, etc.)
- Were there challenges at school? (Learning disabilities, bullying, etc.)
- Did your peers influence you positively or negatively? (Heartbreaks, gang affiliation, etc.)

3. How was life when you finally moved out on your own?

- How old were you?
- What challenges did you face?
- Did you maintain relationships with family members or become alienated?

4. What adversities came with adulthood?
- Were you married? Divorced? Single?
- Do you have children? Do you have a good relationship with them?
- What struggles have you faced?

5. What kinds of jobs have you held?

- Do you have special training?
- What was your favorite job? Least favorite?
- Have you chosen not to work or been unable to work?

6. What losses have you suffered in your life?
- Did you lose someone to death, divorce, or other separation?
- Have you struggled with loss of abilities or other major changes?

SECTION TWO

The Role of Conflict in Your Triumph Story

"The harder the conflict, the more glorious the Triumph."
-Thomas Paine

We often think of "the good life" as being free of trouble, hardship, injustice, or pain, but when authors write a novel, screenplay, or short story, *the adversity that the central character faces is essential*. There is no discovery or growth without it. Can you think of one movie or book where there wasn't some great conflict to be resolved by the end?

Conflict is what moves the story forward and captivates the reader to turn the pages of a book or an audience to watch a movie. The famous actor, Nicolas Cage, stated, "I think what makes people fascinating is conflict; it's drama; it's the human condition. Nobody wants to watch perfection."

As the protagonist in your story, you make the key decisions that affect the plot, primarily influencing the story and propelling it forward. You are the character who faces the most significant obstacles! Battling against tragedies, villains, or seemingly insurmountable situations is what *MAKES* someone a hero. Notice, it says, "battling against adversity" not just "going through adversity."

Bravely confronting the challenges of your life
in and of itself is heroic.

Adversity is without question one of the most powerful forces in life. It can bring out *your best or your worst*. Which one, is up to you. Will the roadblocks you come across make you better or bitter? The most common reaction to Adversity is to recoil and *want it gone*. But the reality is that if you could take away adversity, you would also remove one of *the most important ingredients to greatness.*

*"Circumstances do not make you what you are...
they reveal what you are."* - John C. Maxwell

A few years ago, I was having debilitating migraines almost daily that kept me pretty much bedridden. They were so painful that I went to the ER a few times to see if I had a tumor. They gave me medication that helped the pain for a few hours, but that's all the relief I got. Some days were too painful even to get up go to the hospital! I wanted someone to just chop off my head where it hurt!

What was worse than the migraines was the lack of productivity from just laying in bed all day. I'm a project person so doing nothing was very hard for me.

I have developed a belief that I have to learn something to be able to move on to the next trial. I meditated for days on what I was supposed to learn from these migraines so I could move on.

After pondering it for a while a thought came to my mind. Maybe I needed to learn to be okay with being still, just to be me, not doing anything.

That was a hard concept for me, the overachiever, but it was the lesson I had to grasp. Once I knew what I needed to learn, I worked hard on just being, not a "person doing", but a "human being"!

It took me some time but that mental shift helped me to learn to be comfortable in my own skin, without having to always succeed in life .

I needed that shift in how I looked at my adversity. It has helped me so much in life! My migraines are more manageable now, thanks to this bit of knowledge and some diet changes.

"A successful man is one who can lay a firm foundation with the bricks others have thrown at him." - David Brinkley

You don't have to like Conflict, and you certainly don't have to enjoy it, but if you embrace adversity and trust the role it plays in molding your heroic story, weaknesses will turn into strengths and give you the essential opportunity for growth. "There is something powerful about adversity that has the ability to imprint in our memory, shaping our character, and molding our behavior for the future." -Jim Haudan, CEO of *Root Inc.*

As you strive to see the value in adversity, being able to face and grow from the conflict in your life-story becomes easier and more rewarding. In the words of Henry Ford, "When everything seems to be going against you, remember that an airplane takes off against the wind, not with it." We must have resistance to fly!

"Life shrinks or expands in proportion to one's courage."
-Anais Nin

Resilience Chart

1. In the graph below, list your times of conflict or difficulty that you have survived or overcome.
2. Rate their severity on a scale of one to ten compared to your other trials.
3. Fill in the squares next to your conflicts according to their severity.

(Some examples of conflicts are: being misunderstood as a child, enduring or leaving an unhealthy relationship, losing someone you love, making a change that was difficult, etc.)

Time of Difficulty	1	2	3	4	5	6	7	8	9	10
Example: Death of an elderly loved one (Severity of 8)	▨	▨	▨	▨	▨	▨	▨	▨		

Section Two Assignments

After Filling in your Resilience Chart on the previous page:

1. Fill in your **Past & Present Conflict worksheets** on the following pages.

2. Then, using your **Resilience Chart** and **Past & Present Conflict worksheets** as inspiration, create a piece of art depicting **your Resilience.**

(**Examples of materials to use:** watercolor, markers, ink, acrylic paints, colored pencil, cut-out colored paper, creative lettering, collage or other glued elements, 3D effects, etc.)

PAST CONFLICT

Describe a past conflict that you have been through:

Have you overcome this obstacle yet? If so, how? If not, what do you think is holding you back?

What wisdom and strength have you gained from this challenge?

PAST CONFLICT

Describe a past conflict that you have been through:

Have you overcome this obstacle yet? If so, how? If not, what do you think is holding you back?

What wisdom and strength have you gained from this challenge?

PRESENT CONFLICT

Describe a present conflict in your life:

How do you anticipate overcoming this obstacle?

What wisdom and strength do you believe you will obtain from this challenge?

PRESENT CONFLICT

Describe a present conflict in your life:

How do you anticipate overcoming this obstacle?

What wisdom and strength do you believe you will obtain from this challenge?

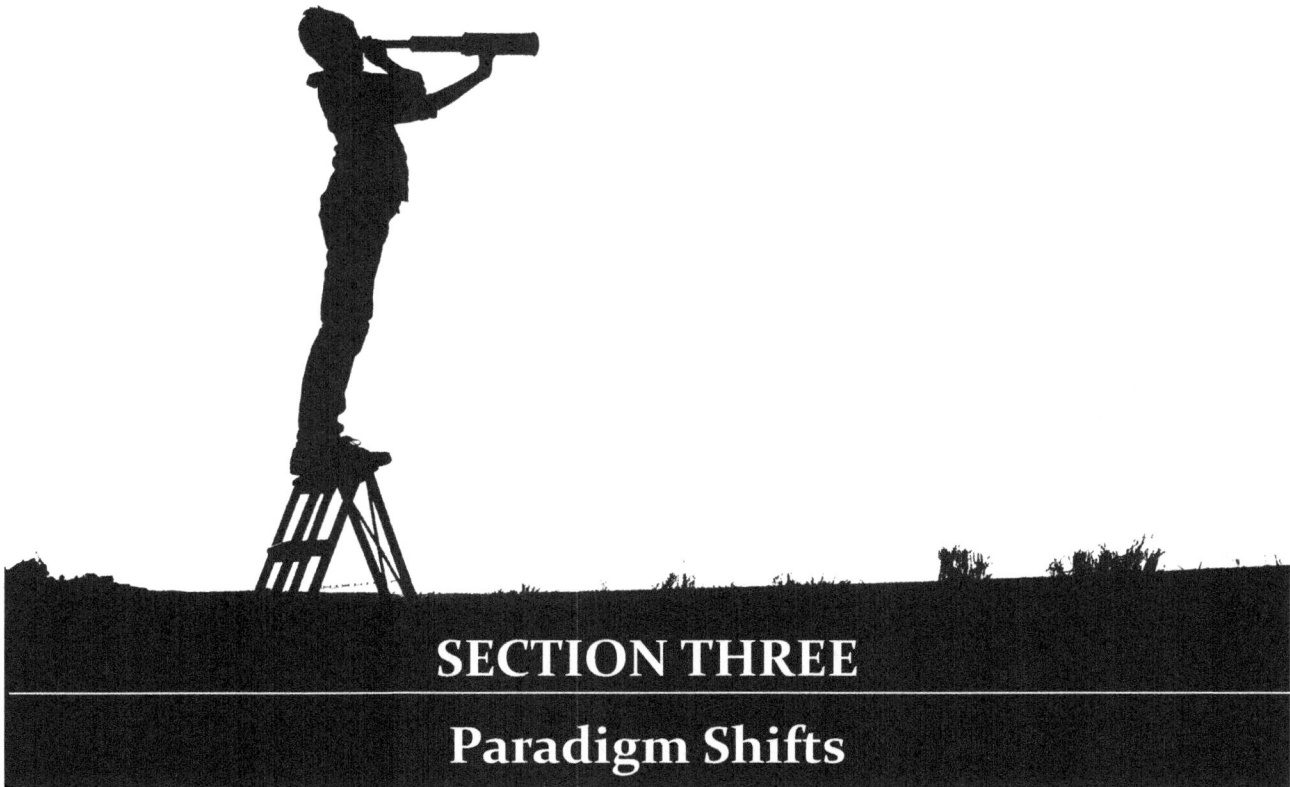

SECTION THREE

Paradigm Shifts

*"**F**ear has two meanings, **F**orget **E**verything **A**nd **R**un, or **F**ace **E**verything **A**nd **R**ise. **The choice is yours."** - Zig Ziglar*

We all have a **Paradigm**. This is the lens through which we interpret the world and perceive reality. The truth is that most of our Paradigm is programmed into our subconscious through the experiences of life, which can be negative or positive. Just like a computer, we have a type of "inner hard drive" from which our ability to process and understand life is centered.

From birth to seven years old, our brain waves are operating in what's referred to as theta and delta modes. These are the low, slow waves that can be seen through brain imaging in reduced consciousness, daydreaming, relaxation, and feeling, rather than during thinking, focused brain activity. The work of a child's brain is to absorb and learn from examples "how to function in the world." This becomes the unconscious programming that directs us throughout our lives. It is influenced most during these formative years when the brain is in this pliable state.

A child growing up who is continually being told he isn't good enough will often adopt that belief deep in the subconscious. Unchecked, it can drive how he thinks and acts as he becomes a teen and adult. In his mind, he's always trying to measure up but never feeling good enough because of how solidly that belief was programmed during the years when the "inner hard drive" was being developed.

When we experience traumas and conflict, which was the focus of *Section Two*, our Paradigm is also affected and feelings of fear, anger, and worry may color our perception as we constantly brace for the next painful experience. Viewing life from this lens can lead to even more pain and difficulty, which are entirely avoidable. The key is to *CONSCIOUSLY PROGRAM* your inner-processor through intention and habit.

"The situation you live in doesn't have to live in you."
-Roberta Flack

To put it more simply, we *CAN* alter our concept of reality using a Paradigm that is optimistic and empowering. We can *choose* to focus on the positive side of life which will decrease our exposure to the negative and create a better reality for ourselves. The principle that **we can be the author of our lives and destiny** begins with *SHIFTING* our Paradigms away from the pre-programming which is destructive, whether from early years or the traumatic effects left by Conflict, towards the miraculous results of *choosing to be positive*.

The Butterfly Analogy

When a caterpillar goes into its cocoon, it first breaks down until it is **almost nothing** but a jelly substance that's called, "imaginal cells. These cells build themselves into the butterfly cells until they have transformed into a full butterfly that can come out of its cocoon and **fly.**

Sometimes in life, I feel like a caterpillar in my cocoon, broken down into **almost nothing**. I just have to remember, that is where I can form my wings to **fly.**

Difficult situations can give us wings. When I was homeless following an abusive situation and had to farm out my children because I didn't want them to be homeless, I felt I had broken down to almost nothing. While homeless I asked myself, *What if I die out here? What will I have given my kids and the world?* That is when I compiled and published my first book... a poetry book. It has precious beliefs, truths, and knowledge of how to get through hard times in it. It is the gift I want to give my kids and the world.

Homelessness gave me the wings to fly and publish my book. Without homelessness, I would probably not have accomplished it. I had been worried about so many things that kept me from publishing it before. Homelessness gave me the courage and momentum to put my book out into the world. **That was my butterfly moment!**

"If things go wrong, don't go with them." - Roger Babson

You begin to control your thoughts when you learn to recognize when and how often you are angry, fearful, or worrying. As you develop this awareness, strive to replace negative thoughts with good ones. One of the best replacements for worry is its opposite: **Gratitude**. If you are worrying, think of things you appreciate which are positive in your life. You can always find them when you look. Often, many blessings may need to be counted to have a profound effect on worry. Keeping a notebook or gratitude journal nearby is an effective way to record the abundant positive things in your life, where you can write and re-read them as often as you feel anxiety creeping in.

Research has proven that being grateful improves both our mental and physical well-being and can have a remarkably positive effect on relationships with those around us. ***PRACTICING*** **Gratitude** can actually *rewire* our brains and be life-changing. "Practicing" is a keyword. Gratitude isn't a state of being; it's something we can and should practice as often as possible because of the power it contains.

In her article, *Practice Being Grateful and Reap the Benefits*, Carla Clark, Ph.D. shares a study where the participants kept a daily **Gratitude Journal** for two weeks. The results were substantially *increased self-esteem* and an *optimistic attitude* about the future. Participants reported *better sleep*, *fewer health issues,* and *increased alertness*.

Clark shares, "Experiencing gratitude can also have a profound effect on our memories. Gratitude practice has shown not only to *increase the recall of positive memories,* having a dash of Gratitude when recalling unpleasant memories can help us *better emotionally process* the negative events, thus bringing emotional closure to these incidents." The list of benefits from taking the time to **be grateful every day** is long and impressive.

"Staying Positive does not mean that things will always turn out okay.
Rather, it is knowing that
YOU will be okay no matter how things turn out."

I was going through a divorce and difficult custody battle for my small girls, trying to get them away from their father who had abused them. My oldest daughter, age five, was still going through therapy for PTSD from the trauma she suffered with him. This custody battle lasted two years.

It had the makings to be a dismal time for me. In fact, I was getting depressed. But I heard something on a TV talk show about using a grateful journal to improve your life, so I began to write five things I was grateful for each day before bedtime. Each "grateful" had to be different than what I had written before.

During the day, I found myself looking for the good so I could gather at least five positive things, and because I was looking, I would always find them.

Writing Gratefuls helped me to heal somehow. My days became lighter and brighter as I focused on the good things! I was able to enjoy those days with my kids. It became easier to be happy. My life had light in the darkness!

Section Three Assignment

Butterfly Moment: Write about a Butterfly Moment/Paradigm Shift that you've had.. (Hint—Sometimes a Butterfly Moment is just a moment till you write it down and you find your wings in the process.) If you can't remember a Butterfly Moment, just write down a moment of difficulty and look for your resilience or any good that has come from it. Let others in your group help you if you would like.

My Butterfly Moment

Gratitude Assignment: Space is provided in this section of the workbook to create two lists.

1. The first one is entitled **Things I am Grateful to have in My Life.** Free-write for five minutes **EVERY DAY** this week without stopping or editing. Write the first things that come to your mind, whether they are big ideas, like having enough to eat, or mundane thoughts such as being able to hit send on your phone and having photos miraculously appear on your friend's phone. Try to reach beyond the obvious, though they may be the first ones you list, and search for the hidden gifts in life you may have been overlooking. A hidden gift may be having a friend listen to your problem or the use of a talent you are discovering.

2. The second list is entitled **Things I am Grateful not to have in My Life.** Write on this list for at least five minutes **EVERY DAY** this week. This list will require creativity as you'll need to think outside your current life and explore all of the challenges you **DON'T HAVE** which would make it so much harder. Imagine if you had the old-fashioned phone your grandmother used as a teen with a six-foot cord in the middle of the kitchen. (I'm grateful **not to have** that!) We can learn to be grateful for the things that don't happen as much as those that do!

Things I'm Grateful to have in my Life	Things I'm Grateful NOT to have in my life

Things I'm Grateful to have in my Life	Things I'm Grateful NOT to have in my life

Things I'm Grateful to have in my Life	Things I'm Grateful NOT to have in my life

Things I'm Grateful to have in my Life	Things I'm Grateful NOT to have in my life

Things I'm Grateful to have in my Life	Things I'm Grateful NOT to have in my life

More Gratitude Pages are available in the Appendix.

Things I'm Grateful to have in my Life	Things I'm Grateful NOT to have in my life

Things I'm Grateful to have in my Life	Things I'm Grateful NOT to have in my life

SECTION FOUR
Circle of Control

"Afflictions color our lives. You choose the color."
- Dr. John C. Maxwell

In Viktor Frankl's memoir, **Man's Search for Meaning**, he describes life in the infamous Nazi death camp, Auschwitz. During his time there, Frankl realized that we cannot avoid suffering. In his book, he shares this important wisdom, *"Everything can be taken from a man but one thing: the last of the human freedoms – to choose one's attitude in any given set of circumstances, to choose one's own way."*

Frankl learned that it was futile to focus on things that were out of his control. He could not change that he was a prisoner, that he had little to eat, and that he might die there. He knew that if he focused on these things, it would only leave him frustrated and angry. Instead, his focus was on what he could control...his attitude. This gave him power.

That is the power you can have! Put all your energy into what you *CAN* control and stop focusing on what you *CAN'T*. Imagine how much you could do if you stopped pushing against the solid bricks of unyielding walls and pushed, instead, against the doors that will open. Imagine how many more doors will open for you!

A **Circle of Control** represents what you have the ability to change. Those things that you can control fall within the circle, for example: what you choose to do, how you react, what you think about, and your attitude. Notice that you can only control yourself.

59

Outside of your Circle of Control are all the things you don't have the ability to change such as how tall you are, the weather, your family, death, what other people do, and even your own past decisions. You free yourself when you let go of these. If you struggle with anger, you don't need to let other people's decisions trigger you. Their actions fall outside your Circle of Control. Don't let others choose how you will act by reacting.

This is your challenge: *Focus on those things within your* Circle of Control *so you retain your inner power, the power to control your life!*

The most important emotion you CAN CONTROL is **Forgiveness**. In many ways, forgiving someone who has deeply hurt you may seem counter-intuitive to justice. When a person has caused you great harm, especially if it is intentional, why would they deserve your Forgiveness? Our sense of fairness creates an impulsive feeling that they must pay for the wrong they have done. However, holding anger and resentment towards someone is not actually exacting a fair punishment. It's only hurting you. This is an important yet difficult insight we should come to recognize. Forgiveness doesn't mean we have to trust the other person; it means letting go and not allowing it to prevent our future growth.

Guilt and lack of Forgiveness towards one's self can be the most debilitating condition of all, which is just as senseless as holding grudges against our enemies.

After leaving my abusive husband, Chris, who tried to kill me and abused my children, I felt such anger towards him that, at times, I even wished him dead! He never had to answer for his crimes. I wanted him to suffer for what he did. I felt like he was a monster and not human!

But, instead of him suffering, I suffered from my lack of forgiveness. When I would think of him, it ruined my mood and sometimes even my day. I also had nightmares about him.

I tried and tried to forgive Chris, but kept grabbing back that anger toward him. I finally took it to my God and prayed to let it go. After all, Chris belonged to Him. I let him be human, not a monster, and let him go.

After that, I felt such relief! I felt lighter, like a burden had been raised off of me. I had no idea how heavy that burden was until it was lifted. What a release! Now I was free to go about my life, not thinking of him.

I heard once, when you can wish someone well, then you know you have forgiven them. I can now say that I wish Chris well. I don't ever want to see him and I don't trust him, but I hope that wherever he is, he's living a better life and improving himself. I hope he has learned how to love.

*"To forgive is to set a prisoner free
and discover that the prisoner was you."*
- Lewis B. Smedes

I had an epiphany while researching the **Circle of Control.** when I saw on someone else's paper and outside their circle of control, were the words "My past decisions."

Wow, I've beaten myself up for years over past decisions! "If only I hadn't made that mistake." "If only I had said this instead of that." "If only I learned the first time around." I said I'm sorry and tried to recompense, but I was still continually wishing I'd done differently.

I realized that sometimes you have to set your past free!

When I farmed out my kids to different family members, I no longer had control over how they were being raised. I wanted them to be treated as I would treat them. I even fervently lectured their caregivers on this. It was to no avail. They were going to raise them during the two years that I was homeless the way they wanted to raise them. I hesitantly stopped trying to control what I couldn't control. I started focusing on the few things that were in my power.

While homeless, couch surfing, I found most things outside my Circle of Control, but I was surprised at the number of things within my control: my attitude, making it by bus or bicycle to my appointments and the store, what my priorities were, how I spoke to people, how I stood up for myself, and whether I tried to stay clean.

When I focused on these things, I felt less anxious, and able to face life's challenges. *I made it through!*

61

OUTSIDE MY CONTROL

I will let go of:

Someone who's caused me pain

Death

My past decisions

MY CIRCLE OF CONTROL

I will focus on:

Forgiveness   How I React

Fill in the CIRCLE OF CONTROL with things you can control.
Around the outside of it, write things you can't control. Some examples are provided.

SECTION FIVE
Believing You Can Achieve

*"Beliefs are choices. First you choose your beliefs.
Then your beliefs affect your choices."*
- Roy T. Bennett

Authoring your life story ahead of time and then seeing that *Triumphant Vision* come true sounds great, doesn't it! But do you believe it's actually possible, or that it's just a gimmicky concept to write about? Before you continue any further in planning your story, it is critical to understand this very simple truth: *you can only achieve what you believe!*

What you believe to be possible influences absolutely every aspect of your life, from how you interpret events to the way you perceive the world around you. Your beliefs form your expectations; they shape and even change your memories! Belief is the perspective through which every experience is filtered. The influence of what you do or don't believe to be possible is so critical, that it is at the core of your reality. Therefore, if you don't believe something to be true or possible, it never will be!

The most powerful method of developing belief strong enough to make your dreams and life plans a reality is to carefully observe the examples of others who have accomplished something that may seem unattainable to you.

For example, from the time running for speed was clocked, it was believed impossible for the human body to run a mile in less than four minutes. This was the widely accepted barrier of what was attainable for humans and remained so until 1954 when Roger Banister proved that theory wrong. Within a year of his achievement, 37 runners broke this perceived barrier, and the year after that, it was beaten by 300 more runners. This story shows that the inspiration provided by others can have a powerful effect on what we, ourselves, believe to be possible and our ability to reach further is heightened as we follow their examples.

When I was dealing with a meth addiction, I had a hard time believing in myself. I kept telling myself how bad I was for having the addiction in the first place. I told myself that I was too far gone to be of any worth to anyone. That made me think even worse of myself!

I voluntarily put myself through drug rehab after drug rehab. After a while I realized that there are some things you just can't shake off! Addiction was beyond my own willpower! I had to seek help from my higher power.

With that help, I was able to see myself with a different perspective, a kinder one. I gained a glimpse of hope. I realize, now, that hope is an important part of achieving. I started to see that I wasn't worth any less; I just had more dirt to be washed off than ever before. I began to have a small inkling that I could overcome this, and that if I could do this hard thing, I could do anything!

It took years, but I was finally able to get clean and stay clean! I always told myself that if I got clean, I would write books and give speeches to groups of people, telling them that they can achieve the seemingly impossible! I know it because I was able to do it.

Section Five Assignments

Read three short stories from *The Triumph Book* featuring people who have risen from their tragedies to find new meaning and purpose in life. Simply observing the rise of the human spirit, no matter the cause for suffering, can be awe-inspiring!

1. As you read these stories, notice how your perspective is changing. Answer the questions in this section of the workbook for each of the three stories you have chosen.

2. Write down your own Paradigm Shifts for your own situations on the worksheet found on page 69.

Story/ Book Title:

What is the tragedy?

What service or new ability was discovered by the Main Character to be used for the benefit of others?

What choices or actions helped the Main Character find purpose or joy?

Story/ Book Title:

What is the tragedy?

What service or new ability was discovered by the Main Character to be used for the benefit of others?

What choices or actions helped the Main Character find purpose or joy?

Story/ Book Title:

What is the tragedy?

What service or new ability was discovered by the Main Character to be used for the benefit of others?

What choices or actions helped the Main Character find purpose or joy?

Perspective Shifts

Through this process, have you had any **Shifts in Perspective** on your own challenges?

SECTION SIX
Supporting Characters

"A friend knows the song in my heart and sings it to me when my memory fails." - Donna Roberts

Rarely do you read a book where the Main Character is going through their challenges alone. In almost every story, there are **Supporting Characters**. Likewise, you have Supporting Characters in your life. Your family, friends, neighbors, and even the people you meet by chance can all be Supporting Characters in the story of your life. Whether they are positive or negative influences, they help shape you into the person you become.

It's through others that you learn about yourself. Everyone has qualities that they can't see in a mirror. Being around others is like looking into a different type of mirror. They can help you see the qualities you may have which could be good qualities such as bravery, compassion, or a sense of humor. Negative traits can also be mirrored back to you by those around you. It is said that if something irritates you about a person, it might be a sign that you possess it's what you need to change in yourself. Examples of traits we dislike in others that we often carry ourselves can be things such as pride or jealousy.

You learn from others: who you want and don't want to be like. If a family member or friend was kind and gentle with you, these are often strengths you strive to obtain. On the other hand, being berated or bullied might help you carefully avoid treating others that way. Everyone has something they don't want to repeat when they have children

You learn from experience how to love and be loved, what it takes to feel important, how to learn, and how to get the support you need. The treatment you got from others often affects your behavior. These experiences color your Perception of reality.

If your environment is negative, you can learn how to break through it with the help of others. If it is positive, you are uplifted and encouraged by their enthusiasm. Friends and mentors can give you strength, courage, and wisdom.

My best friend, Leta, stayed close to me even through my meth addiction and homelessness. We had been neighbors long before I ever became addicted. Our children met first, and then introduced us to each other. We became close friends and even when Leta moved an hour away, we would still get together once a week. We had the best times together!

When I was in my addiction, Leta would talk to me on the phone. Somehow, she was able to perceive when I had used meth recently. She told me, "That's not you. I know the real you! You can make it back. I believe in you!"

Her gentle, loving words were just the ones I needed to hear! It gave me hope and wisdom that I needed to know in order to get back to my real self. It gave me

It is important to spend time around people you want to be like, who you want to emulate, and those who have positive character traits. It's also important to not be around people who tear you down or do things that you don't like. It doesn't make you judgmental or snotty to do this. You're just setting boundaries, sticking up for yourself, and creating an environment in which to thrive. Anyone who criticizes you for doing this probably shouldn't be counted among your friends.

The more you surround yourself with people you want to be like, the more you will be able to become whom you want to be. Be picky and selective about whom you spend time with or you will remain stuck. *Just a few good friends are much better than many that don't meet your requirements.*

Just before I came out of my abusive marriage with Chris, Leta gave me this bit of wisdom:

"It's sad when a giver gets hooked up with a taker. Givers need to be with givers, not takers!"

From her advice and my negative experience with Chris, I decided to be more careful about who I chose to be around and who I chose for my friends.

I created a list for myself with the traits I wanted in a friend. Here are some examples of criteria on my list:

- They are uplifting and don't put me down.
- They are honest.
- They have time for me .

Everyone has their own needs from friends. Another person might have totally different requirements on their list.

With this list, I made a chart. I wrote in my friends' names and checked each trait that they matched. Those that didn't have many matches, I decided to spend less time with. Those who matched a lot of them, I decided to spend more time with.

There is a similar chart on the upcoming pages for you to fill out with your requirements and friends' names.

Note: Leta died from cancer a few years ago. Still, her gentle kind words and wisdom resound clearly in my mind.

FRIENDSHIP REQUIREMENT LIST

- In the table below, under the requirements column, write the qualities that you want in a friend.
- Then in the columns labeled "Friends Names" list your friends.
- Now, put an "X" in the check boxes, under each name, for every requirement they meet.

#	Requirements in order to be my friend:
1	Example : They must be honest and trustworthy. (They don't lie to me,)
2	Example : They must be kind. (They don't put me down.)
3	
4	
5	
6	
7	
8	
9	
10	
11	
12	
13	
14	
15	

"Be careful who your friends are
you will become like them."

Friends Names:

	×	×	×	×	×	×	×	×	×	×	×	×	×	×	×	×	×

Lastly, put your own name on your list. You will find more friends that meet your requirements if you do too.

Supporting Characters from your life

Name two Supporting Characters in your life and write about the gift of strength, courage, and/or wisdom they have given you.

Name	
Relationship	

Name	
Relationship	

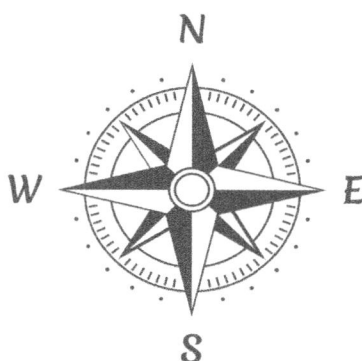

SECTION SEVEN

Finding Your Mission

"If you have built castles in the air, your work need not be lost; that is where they should be. Now put the foundation under them." – Thoreau

When writing a story, your Main Character *MUST* have a purpose. People don't read books about someone who wanders around aimlessly. The hero is always on a mission to solve a mystery, find something or someone, or become greater than who they were at the beginning. They have a purpose that is at the core of their story. To see the protagonist achieve his or her goals and overcome the obstacles along the way is the reason you keep reading!

You are discovering and writing your personal story as you live it. Having a well-defined Mission will help you live on purpose and "be the author of your destiny." Many successful people who've achieved great things in life have carefully written **Personal Mission Statements** that serve as their map, their compass, or **True North**.

Compasses work by directing you to what is called "Magnetic North" which is actually a point in the arctic regions of Canada that constantly shifts location as the earth's magnetic fields fluctuate. Fluid iron in the core of our planet creates a magnetic field that pulls in the direction of north, however, if you truly want to reach the top of the earth, and not land somewhere in the Canadian arctic, you actually need to use "True North."

In navigation, it is easy to move between two points if you know the terrain and the distance is relatively short. In our personal lives, however, this is rarely the case. The challenges of everyday life can make it easy to get lost, sidetracked, disoriented, tired and confused. Thankfully, you can find peace in the midst of life's chaos by having a fixed destination upon which you can put your faith and trust, knowing that no matter how rough the seas around you become, you can steer your ship exactly where it needs to sail.

A **Personal Mission Statement** defines what contributions you want to make in the world. It speaks of your passions, your strengths, talents, and how you will serve or influence others. It can change as you grow throughout life and find more of your purpose. It should be short and succinct. Its purpose is to be that "True North" point that you steer towards. No matter what happens, knowing your destination gives you the confidence to keep moving forward as you journey through life.

When my kids and I were split up, I found my previous mission statement derailed. All I wanted to do was be a good mom to my kids. They were my mission.

I found myself looking for new meaning in life. I have a strong relationship with them as adults, but they have their own lives now. They can't be my mission anymore.

I've always had a talent and passion for illustrating and writing. Along the way, I also gained a passion for speaking in public. This was a strength I had to learn. In fact, I am an introvert and speaking is an extroverted thing, so I joined a public speaking club that taught me how to give inspiring presentations. I knew I wanted to share my strength, hope, and light with the world, so I developed my new mission statement:

"To touch as many people as I can with my strength, hope, and light through my talents that make their hearts smile."

How to Write a Personal Mission Statement

A **Mission Statement** should define how you want to live and what you would like to achieve. This will empower you to have such clarity that success is assured. Mission Statements are generalized declarations of your values and the "big picture" achievements you wish to make. They are not specific plans... *those are GOALS and we will talk about in the next section.*

1. First, think of up to three things you are passionate about. Write these on the next page.

2. Go back through your **Strengths Inventory** on page 10 and put **an arrow** next to five strengths you feel are most important for your life's mission. Also, write these on the next page. (These don't have to be your top five. They don't even have to be strengths that you currently have, but ones that you value and want to gain.)

3. Using your passions and your five important strengths, write a **Mission Statement** embodying these passions, values, and strengths as the goal of your life.

Here are a few good examples of Mission Statements from famous people:

"My mission in life is not merely to survive, but to thrive; and to do so with some passion, some compassion, some humor, and some style." - Maya Angelou, author

"I shall not fear anyone on Earth. I shall fear only God. I shall not bear ill will toward anyone. I shall not submit to injustice from anyone. I shall conquer untruth by truth. And in resisting untruth, I shall put up with all suffering." - Mahatma Gandhi, political and religious leader

"To use my gifts of intelligence, charisma, and serial optimism to cultivate the self-worth and net-worth of women around the world." - Amanda Steinberg, founder of Dailyworth.com

"Living a balanced life means nurturing the academic, physical, and spiritual aspects of my life so I can maintain a sense of well-being and self-esteem." – Denise Morrison, CEO of Campbell Soup Company

More examples:

"To make my decisions based on my true beliefs, work on improving myself each day, and sculpt my life into a masterpiece."

"To live boldly, using my love for other countries and languages, and Charismatic nature to be a leader in foreign diplomacy."

"Use my talents to uplift and serve others, becoming true giver in life."

"Live with determination to overcome challenges and use them to become stronger."

"to use my gentle nature and love for children to teach and touch the lives of as many children as I possibly can."

"Take nothing for granted. Be kind, be humble, be grateful. Make the most out of every minute."

"to value my family, making life decisions based on how they will help each family member, and homeschool my children to give them the best start I can."

Mission Statement Prep

Before you write a Mission Statement, it might help to ask yourself these questions:

What are you passionate about?

What difference do you want to make in the world?

How can you use your strengths & talents (or strengths you want to gain) to make that difference?

Now that you've had some self discovery and insight into your future life, contemplate how you can make the most out of your life (in whatever form that takes for you). Use your answers to write your Mission Statement on the following **Mission Statement worksheet.**

Your Personal Mission Statement

You do not
DECIDE
your future.
you decide your
HABITS
and your habits
*decide your **FUTURE.***"

~ Donte' A. Bundrent

SECTION EIGHT

Charting Your Course

With a clearly defined **Mission Statement**, the next step in achieving your **TRIUMPHANT FUTURE** is to break down your vision into measurable and achievable steps. This gives you control to move ahead intentionally towards your aspirations. These steps are often referred to as "**Goals**."

Goal setting requires specific, actionable procedures which are clearly defined. It is important to put a time frame to your Goals, knowing that we aren't always able to reach them exactly as planned; but having deadlines creates the opportunity to shoot for the stars and hit the moon...the end result is that you still left the earth's atmosphere and are that much closer to your destination.

Goals should be measurable and detailed. For example, "I want to lose weight" is a much weaker Goal than saying, "I want to lose weight by exercising six days a week and cutting out sugar. I plan to lose 10 pounds in two months." This Goal meets all the requirements of effective Goal setting because it states what you will do, how you will do it, and by when.

 Goals should be **S.M.A.R.T**:

    Specific- describe exactly what you what to achieve.
    Measurable- you'll know when you've met your goal.
    Achievable– they are reasonable keeping your abilities in mind.
    Relevant– they line up with your **Mission Statement.**
    Time Delineated- there is a set time frame.

Periodically, you should evaluate your Goals, decide if you stuck to the plan properly and, if so, determine if it was successful or not. If the Goals you set didn't bring the ultimate planned outcome, you can conduct an assessment of what was not working as expected and make adjustments for the next round of Goal setting. Remember, life is a learning process and Goals need to be continually created and evaluated as we progress and develop!

My sweet parents taught me about goals at an early age. They had my brothers, sister, and me writing our goals by age seven. I remember writing out our goals for the coming year and putting it in our Christmas stockings to be revealed the next Christmas. Amazingly, when we got the stockings out at Christmastime . The next year, I had always achieved my goals! Later, I learned that when you write a goal down, the subconscious part of the brain works to make it happen. I may not have understood all the particulars, but I continued to write my own goals as I got older.

I saw the importance of improving myself in my early teens. I usually picked goals that would help me see a transformation in myself such as not pestering my brother or trying to learn something everywhere I went. This helped with my depression a little bit.

I remember my dad making a goal to buy a Volvo. In the late seventies, it was his dream car. He put a picture of one on the bathroom mirror. Then he worked hard. He was a financial planner who was pretty much running his own business. It was hard to get high-paying clients, but somehow, he tracked down sufficient clients and made enough money to be able to afford a Volvo. He paid no attention to the color of the car when he chose one. He was amazed to find that the car he picked had the same coloring inside and out as the one he had on the mirror!

I started to set goals like that, cutting pictures from magazines of things that I wanted and either put them in a book or taped them to my wall. I found that making sure I always saw those images helped my subconscious turn them into reality.

Section Eight Assignments

1. Fill in three **Short Term Goals** in the following charts.
2. Fill in three **Long Term Goals** in the following charts.

"The trouble with not having a goal is that you can spend your life running up and down the field and never score."

- Bill Copeland

S.M.A.R.T.
Short Term Goal

SPECIFIC – What exactly is my goal:

RELEVANT - Fits with my vision:	**Yes**	**No**

MEASURABLE - I will know I have met my goal when:

ACHIEVABLE

Actions I must take to meet my goal:

What **skills** I will use or need to accomplish my goal:

Other help or **things** I need to accomplish my goal. (Ex. To do a painting, you need paints.):

TIME DELINEATED - Due Date:	**Completed "X"**	

S.M.A.R.T.
Short Term Goal

SPECIFIC – What exactly is my goal:

RELEVANT - Fits with my vision: | Yes | No

MEASURABLE - I will know I have met my goal when:

ACHIEVABLE

Actions I must take to meet my goal:

What **skills** I will use or need to accomplish my goal:

Other help or **things** I need to accomplish my goal:

TIME DELINEATED - Due Date: | Completed "X"

S.M.A.R.T.
Short Term Goal

SPECIFIC – What exactly is my goal:

RELEVANT - Fits with my vision: | **Yes** | **No**

MEASURABLE - I will know I have met my goal when:

ACHIEVABLE

Actions I must take to meet my goal:

What **skills** I will use or need to accomplish my goal:

Other help or **things** I need to accomplish my goal:

TIME DELINEATED - Due Date: | **Completed "X"** |

Long Term Goal

Specific Goal:

Mini-Goal:

Due Date:

Mini-Goal:

Due Date:

Mini-Goal:

Due Date:

X	Actions

X	Actions

X	Actions

Strengths I will use (Can include strengths you wish to gain):

Other things I will Need (Ex. To be a scientist you need a degree):

Anticipated Completion:

Long Term Goal

Specific Goal:

Mini-Goal:

Due Date:

Mini-Goal:

Due Date:

Mini-Goal:

Due Date:

X	Actions

X	Actions

X	Actions

Strengths I will use (Can include strengths you wish to gain):

Other things I will Need:

Anticipated Completion:

Long Term Goal

Specific Goal:

Mini-Goal:

Due Date:

Mini-Goal:

Due Date:

Mini-Goal:

Due Date:

X	Actions

X	Actions

X	Actions

Strengths I will use (Can include strengths you wish to gain):

Other things I will Need:

Anticipated Completion:

> *"Excellence is not a destination. It's a continuous Journey"*
> - Brian Tracy

SECTION NINE

Character Arcs

> *"To improve is to change; to be perfect is to change often."*
> - Winston Churchill

Character Arcs are essential to every story. They are the measure of how a character changes over time. There are three types of Character Arcs: ascending, descending, and flat. Descending is when the character is moving in a negative direction, becoming worse instead of better, and flat is when a character remains the same, with no dynamic growth to be seen. Since you are writing your **Triumph Story**, the Arc you want is the ascending type, rising to higher levels of your potential, finding greater happiness, purpose, and meaning in life.

Imagine you are climbing up a steep mountain made of ice. As long as you are chipping away at the hardened ice, you can create hand and footholds on which to pull yourself up and continue the climb to the top. If you stop and rest, you will remain in one place. Staying put isn't necessarily "easier" than the climb because, after all, you are stuck on the side of a mountain! If you sit there long enough, the ice will begin to melt from your body heat. Instead of staying in one place, you will actually begin to slide down, going in the opposite direction. Unless you start to chip away at the ice again, making new hand and footholds, you could end up at the very bottom.

Although this is only a metaphor, it is an accurate description of life's journey. We must always be climbing or we will undoubtedly go backward. When it comes to writing a story, a screenplay, *or planning your life*, it is essential to understand that there are three directions in which a character can go, and the Character Arc you WANT for your life, is **Ascending**. Keep chipping away at that mountain of ice, it IS hard work, but *you WILL progress UPWARD!*

As Goals are achieved, changes will be seen and appreciated in the physical world around you; however, the *most valuable transformation* is what happens within the Main Character/Hero who is striving towards these visions. When you have determined your **Mission** and aspire to something greater than you are right now, like the hero in a story, you are taking up your **Quest**. Even little Goals you have made and achieved count as success in your Mission, such as giving a speech, achieving a good grade, or just getting to school or work on time every day.

Each Goal is a "Threshold," a point or level at which something begins or changes. For example, you know that when you cross the threshold of a house, you are no longer outside. Something has changed. A Threshold is about *change*. In the journey of a hero, it is the point at which we gain something new in life; something we want to get; something we want to achieve; something we want to become; a difference we want to make. Standing in the way of your next Threshold (be it big or little) are people or things that can be referred to as "**Threshold Guardians**."

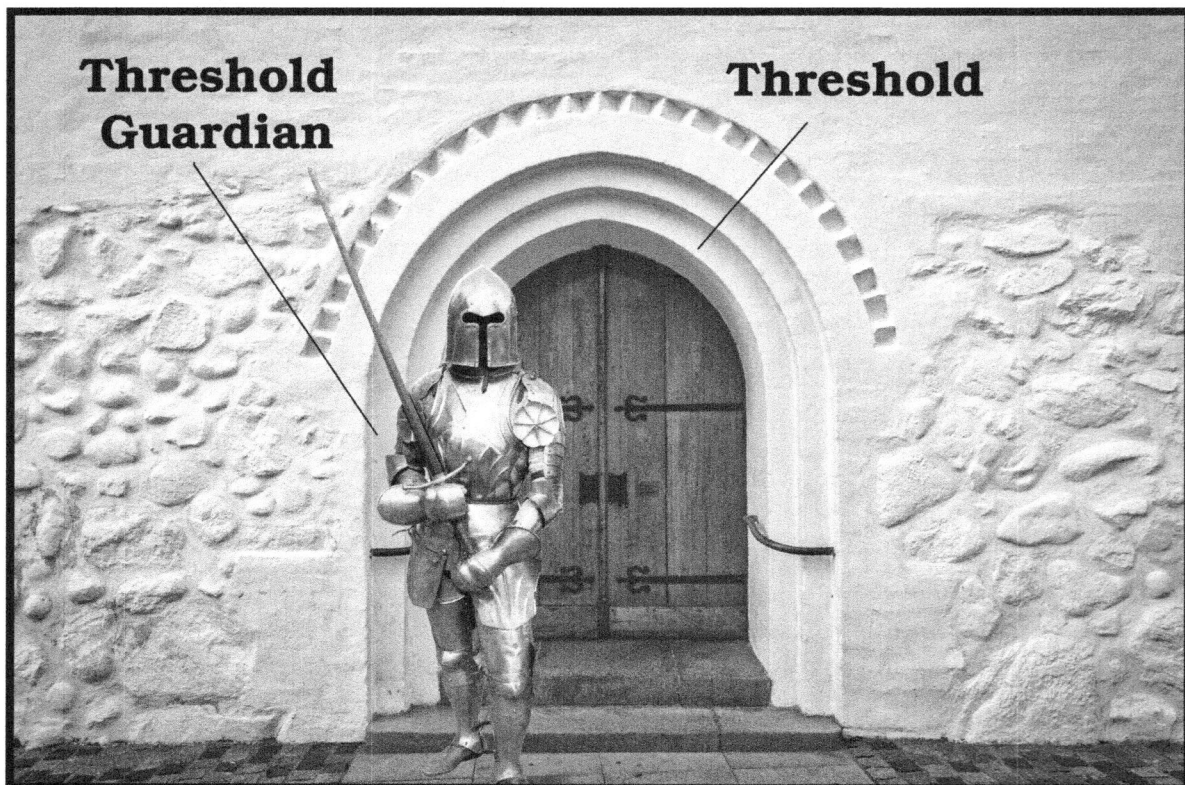

"FAILURES are part of GROWTH.
*If you don't fail, **You'll never LEARN.***
If you don't learn.
*You'll never **GROW***"

Threshold Guardians make it even more difficult to cross that threshold. It is like they are *protecting it,* not allowing you to pass...*until* you have been strengthened by their resistance.

In video games, to "win the game" you must continue to improve and become better at the challenge. This is sometimes referred to as "leveling up." You have to beat, or complete, one level in order to move on to the next. Until you have become good enough to overcome the obstacles of that level, you will remain, continuing to go through it until you have gained enough skills (or points or whatever the measurement is to complete that stage of the game) to move up.

But what happens when you move on to the next level? Does the game ever get easier? If it did, no one would buy or play it! That is because the whole reason you are playing the game is to prove you are skilled, maybe even the best player or a highly ranked one, and that can *ONLY* happen if you are challenged! This is also true in storytelling, and it is especially accurate in life. The stronger you get, the more difficult challenges you are able to take on, and the greater the joy you will experience in accomplishing them!

The time it takes to gain strength can often be confused with "failure." In fact, there is zero growth without what seems like "failure," but *we either win or we learn, we never fail!* Elon Musk, the founder of SpaceX and CEO of Tesla, once said, "There's a silly notion that failure's not an option at NASA. Failure is an option here. If things are not failing, you are not innovating enough."

This truth, that failure is both necessary and good, can be easy to say, but hard to believe. In the midst of our inability to "cross our latest Thresholds" we may feel like nothing is working, that we "aren't good enough" and sometimes we may go so low as to say, "There's no use in trying!" These are the times when our strength is tested the most, and these times will happen... *often!*

It is critical that you *prepare* to face these moments. Being able to see past failure, to recognize it for what it is, can be your **Hero Super Power**! Once your mind is set, firm in the belief that nothing is a failure; that "all things work together for your good," you will become *UNSTOPPABLE*!

So how do you obtain this **Super Power**? Is it as hard to gain as crossing a Threshold? Fortunately, the answer is that this Super Power is within your grasp! Firmly set your mind on the truth that there is no failure by adopting a **Mantra**. Every time you start to disbelieve, a Mantra can immediately stop those negative thoughts.

"If you never give up, you can NEVER BE DEFEATED!"

The concept of Mantra originates from the mystical, where it is centered in spiritual practices like yoga and meditation. It has since been expanded to include the adoption of a personal motivational message that is used repetitively.

When my kids were little, I read an article in a magazine about knowing what you want to be like and acting the part. I helped me come up with this **Mantra**:

> **"I *act* based on who I want to be, rather than *react*, so I can remain *intact*."**

I didn't know how much this phrase would affect my life! When a situation would arise that I might otherwise react to, such as the bus not picking up my child from school, I chose to be calm and forgiving because that's who I wanted to be. I found myself becoming the person I wanted to be more and more and I began to like the person I was becoming.

An added effect of living this way was that I no longer had buttons that could easily be pushed by others to make me react a certain way. I had effectively removed my buttons!

I've written several Mantras since then. I chose each to help me overcome what I was going through. Each made an impact on my life for the better, strengthening me through my trials. They helped me to be a better person.

The word "**Mantra**" can be broken into two halves. "Man" means "mind" and "tra" means to "transport." A Mantra is a vehicle for harnessing the power and potential of the mind using a sound, vibration, or message which is repeated. For the purpose of this program, Mantra will be employed as an inspirational quote that you select, memorize, and hang in a visible place. Repeat your Mantra in moments when your mind becomes discouraged and you are beginning to doubt.

A Mantra serves as a reminder of your intention and beliefs, especially when you need to lend support to yourself. Many important people who have left a lasting legacy in our world have credited their success to a daily Mantra. For example, every morning when he woke up, Steve Jobs asked himself, *If today were the last day of my life, would I want to do what I am about to do today?* Ben Franklin's Mantra was, "What good shall I do today?"

To assist you towards the **TRIUMPH** in your life, a list of many excellent Mantras is provided here. Carefully read them all and pick the one that resonates most with you. You may have certain tendencies which can be addressed specifically with your Mantra, such as worrying, procrastination, or berating yourself.

A Mantra should help you believe in yourself and know that you can accomplish great things. There is also space to write your own Mantra if you would like, using these as inspiration to compose one that says exactly what you want to remind yourself of every day.

Harnessing the Super Power of a Mantra is simple, but "simple" is not the same as "easy." Once a Mantra has been selected, it is up to you to put it to work, every day, especially at times when you are feeling discouraged and considering giving up. It may feel unnatural at first to speak and believe something empowering and positive when your perception is telling you otherwise, but in time it does get easier and as it does, you will see your ability to cross Thresholds increase. It is well worth taking the time to carefully select and make a practice of using a *DAILY* Mantra.

Section Nine Assignment

Circle a Mantra from these options or write a custom Mantra that you will use for the next month (or more... although you can experiment with new Mantras each month until you settle on one that becomes your words-to-live-by).

Then, using paper and an art medium, **creatively write and decorate** your Mantra. Post it in a location where it can be seen regularly.

Mantra List

- **Be a Warrior, Not a Worrier**

- **Don't compare your worst to someone else's best**

- **Tough Times Don't Last; Tough People Do**

- **Things Don't Happen to Me, They Happen for Me**

- **You Didn't Come This Far to Only Come This Far**

- **I Am Capable. I Am Strong. I Believe in Myself!**

- **You Can Find an Excuse or You Can Find a Way**

- **You Get What You Focus On**

- **Kick-Ass, But Be Kind**

- **Respect is given. Trust is earned**

- **Action Conquers Fear**

- **Excellence Does Not Require Perfection**

- **Don't Be Afraid to Be Great**

- **Work hard; play hard**

- **Our Intentions Create Our Reality**

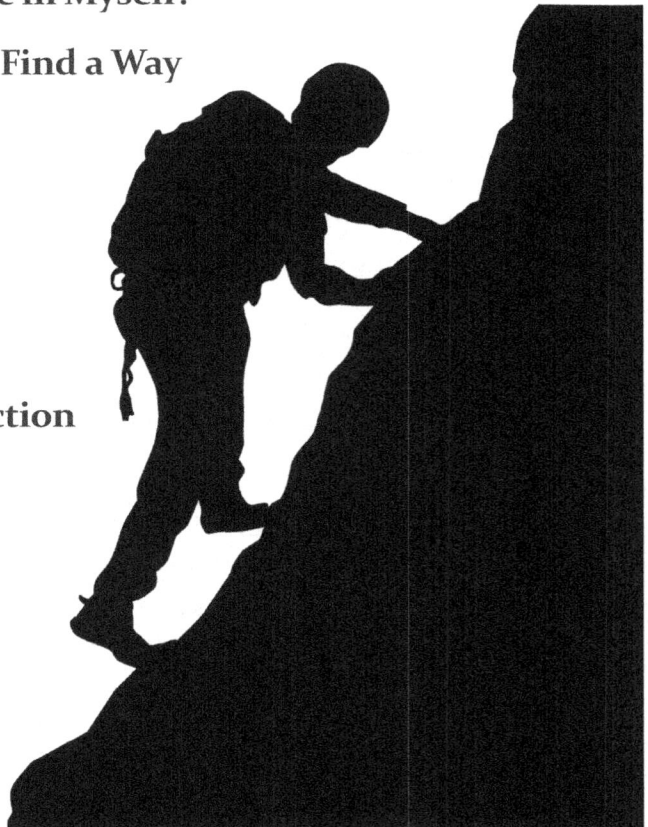

- Know Your Limitations, and Defy Them
- One Year Equals 365 Possibilities
- You Miss 100% of The Shots You Don't Take
- It's The Start That Stops Most People
- The Best Project You'll Ever Work On Is You
- Work Harder
- You can do anything, but not everything
- Do what works for you
- What Would You Attempt to Do If You Knew You Could Not Fail?
- Do what you can; let the rest go
- You've got this!
- I am enough
- Don't be afraid to give up the good and go for the great
- Love radiates out in all directions and returns to me multiplied
- Life is a gift. Enjoy the present
- Where I am right now is exactly where I need to be.
- Optimism is the best way for a right side up life
- My thoughts do not control me, I control my thoughts
- Failure is not final; Mistakes are not fatal!
- Today is a fresh start
- I choose to be proud of myself today
- I give myself permission to be imperfect/ human
- I'm exactly where I'm supposed to be
- Make time for what matters most
- Treasure the moments
- Life is fragile - Handle with care
- What you focus on will expand

- **Find the good in life**
- **Excellence does not require perfection**
- **Grow through what you go through**
- **Everything will be okay in the end; if it's not okay, it's not the end**
- **You've made it through 100% of your days so far**
- **Love is a choice**
- **Failure is part of growth; get back up!**
- **No one can replace you**
- **I matter!**
- **Choose love!**
- **Breathe, Just breathe**
- **Shine**
- **Let go and move on**
- **You can only try, but make it your best try**
- **I will succeed - so there is no need to fear**

Or write your own Mantra:

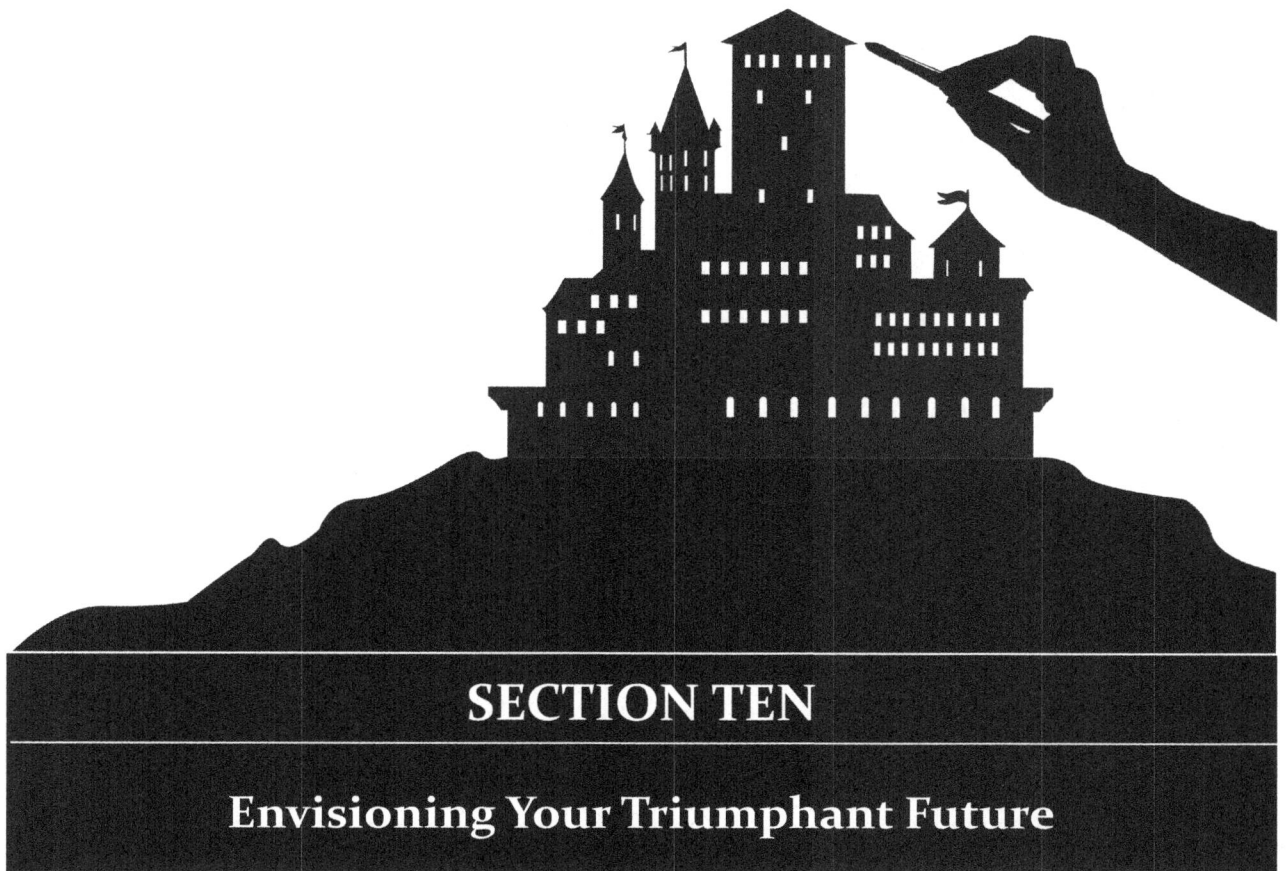

SECTION TEN

Envisioning Your Triumphant Future

Great vision precedes great achievement...When you embrace a vision,
you become focused, energized, and confident.
You know where you're headed, and why you're going there.
-Dr. John C. Maxwell

The tagline of this workbook encourages you to *Discover, Write and LIVE Your Triumph Story*. In the previous sections, you explored who you are, what you have overcome, what matters most to you, what you want to accomplish, and who you want to be. In this final section, you will be given the tools to *ensure your story is Triumphant.* This is the section that will do the most to empower you to LIVE your Triumph Story!

There is a difference between living and **living on purpose**. When just living, we move through life the way it dictates although we may not always notice that is what we are doing. Life often has a way of taking control whether we like it or not, such as when we are going through a difficult Conflict. When we stop setting Goals and having a Mission that calls to us, but instead allow life to direct our day-to-day activities, we are failing to accomplish as much as we can with our time, talents, and energy.

We can *MAKE* our future, not just be surprised by or led aimlessly to it. This is done by having a **Vision** of that future which is deeply implanted in our minds, rehearsed, and visited frequently. When we are faced with the little choices that can either distract or direct us, we are naturally able to choose those things that bring our Vision to reality. *We are that smart!*

Our subconscious mind has the ability to be taught and educated by our conscious mind so that it guides and directs us in the midst of life's chaos to our most desired Goals. The majority of our behavioral and thought patterns are actually directed by the *subconscious mind*, not the conscious. According to Emmanuel Donchin, *Director of the Laboratory for Cognitive Psychophysiology at the University of Illinois,* "As much as 99% of cognitive activity may be non-conscious." As we train our subconscious to know what we seek in life, we are able to tap into the power of intuition, which helps us control all aspects of existence toward our Goals.

What you think about is what you bring about. Creating a clear, solid picture in your mind of your ultimate Goals is a powerful force for ushering those desires into reality. There are two effective tools for harnessing the ability of our minds to bring about the reality we have planned so we can *truly LIVE our Triumph.* The first is to create scenes in our mind where we actually witness what it is like to have our Goals achieved. This is a technique frequently used by athletes who credit their success to practicing in their minds as well as physically.

Lindsey Vonn is a downhill skier who has won multiple World Cups. She says, "I always visualize the run before I do it. By the time I get to the start gate, I've run that race 100 times already in my head, picturing how I'll take the turns."

Olympic Gold Medal swimmer, Missy Franklin says, "When I get there, I've already pictured what's going to happen a million times so I don't actually have to think about it."

Jerry West is a former NBA player who became known as "Mr. Clutch" because of how he could make baskets just as the buzzer was about to go off. West credits his ability to make these big shots under pressure to visualization. He would make that shot countless times in his mind before every game. A long list of celebrities cite visualization as part of their method to reach success including Tiger Woods, Michael Jordan, Jim Carrey, and Oprah, to name a few.

In addition to visualizing in detail your Goals being achieved, you can empower your success by creating a **Vision Board**. The basis of Vision Board success is centered on the principles of the **Law of Attraction.**

There is a heightened emotional vibration associated with those things a person wishes to achieve. If focused on, those vibrations attract into a person's life whatever they desire. When we are able to focus on our Goals by placing the Vision Board where it can be seen often, the power of the mind can translate it into reality. In a world that overwhelms us with negative messages, having *a visual representation of our hopes and dreams* is an encouraging way to help us move in a positive direction.

In the past, the Law of Attraction has been both embraced and criticized; however, science has finally caught up with what success-focused people already know through a new theory known as **Quantum Physics** (also called "Quantum Mechanics"). This is a scientific concept that recognizes all matter at the smallest (quantum) level is vibrating energy and nothing is "fixed." This energy can act or be acted upon by other energies which can include the energy of thought and intention! Previously, our understanding of the universe was based solely on the physics of Newton which states that the universe is made up of solid, unchangeable building blocks. With the discovery of Quantum Physics, we now know that everything at its smallest level is fluid and ever-changing.

Even Einstein is a contributor to the reality of Quantum Physics through his formula e=mc2. This 1905 formula explains the relationship between energy and matter and proves that energy and matter are interchangeable. In reality, everything is energy!

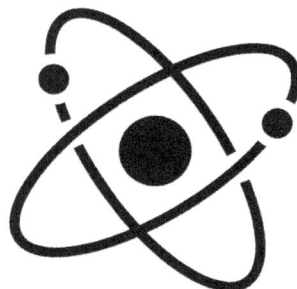

Twelve years ago, when I moved to the town I live in now, I wanted to put the ugly parts of my past behind me. I sought a new chapter of my life. I wanted a season of harmony. I decided to create a **Vision Board** to attract good in my life.

I used a large brightly colored foam board. Then I collected pictures, magazine cut outs, printed some pictures from online, and printed and cut out words to use on my board. I used pictures of things and words that represented the beautiful new life I wanted and the amazing "me" that I wanted to become. These included pictures of my adult children and the grandchildren I wanted to spend more time with, pictures of good friends to remind me of the quality of people I wanted to attract and even the car I wanted to drive.

I put on representations of my entrepreneur goals such as writing and publishing my books, owning a graphic design and illustration business, and to become an inspirational speaker.

I added my spiritual goals: to become more like my God, be true to my faith, enjoy the journey, and be proud to be me. I added sticker words: *Never give up, have courage, believe, shine, and grow.* Then I added embellishments of beautiful stickers and ribbon. I put it on the wall above my bed where I could see it before I fell asleep at night and when I woke up in the morning.

It worked so well that I was accomplished most of what was on the board in a few years. So, I made another one, then one a few years after that. Now I'm working on my fourth Vision Board.

I know Vision Boards assist my subconscious mind to work on the things I want in my life. I'll probably do many more. Life is beautiful now. I've achieved the season of harmony that I asked for!

The activities for this final section are to create vehicles for using the power of your mind to bring your Goals into reality.

Goal Visualization

The first activity is to write a narrative which is a **Detailed Visualization** where you witness in your mind what it will be like to achieve your Goal or Goals. Write it down utilizing all five senses to describe how it feels to reach this achievement. Reread it often to keep that scene continually in your mind.

For example, if your end Goal is to play a starring role in a community play, your vision might look like this:

> Opening night in the auditorium pulsates with enthusiasm while you pace the floor, silently practicing your lines for the last time. As the curtain raises, the roar from the audience is felt as much as heard, rumbling the stage beneath your feet. The crowd disappears into the descending darkness as spotlights envelop and transport you into a universe where you *ARE* the character you have been rehearsing. Words and emotions are instinctive and the hushed audience is transfixed in this fantasy right along with you. At the conclusion of your final monologue, the audience explodes in a standing ovation. The house lights go up revealing the sea of clapping hands and you take a mental snapshot of this moment, cherishing the achievement of a goal you set long ago!

Notice how each detail is vividly written. The inclusion of the senses creates an illusion of being there. Playing the mental movie through from the start to finish often will give you the momentum you need to achieve your Goal.

For more help with writing your Detailed Visualization, see *The Seven Rules of Exceptional Writing* in the Appendix.

Use the next two pages to write your Vision.

A Step Inside My Vision (Goal Visualization)

Vision Board

Using your **Mission Statement & Goals,** create a piece of art on a large poster board. Include inspiring words or phrases and colorful visuals to remind you of the plans you've made during this program. You may also include other things you want in your life.

Materials Required

- Large poster board
- Pictures and/or magazines
- Written, printed, or magazine words
- Tape runner (recommended) or glue stick
- Pens, paint, or other medium

Other Options

- Colored cardstock
- Ribbons
- Drawings
- Stickers
- Other embellishments

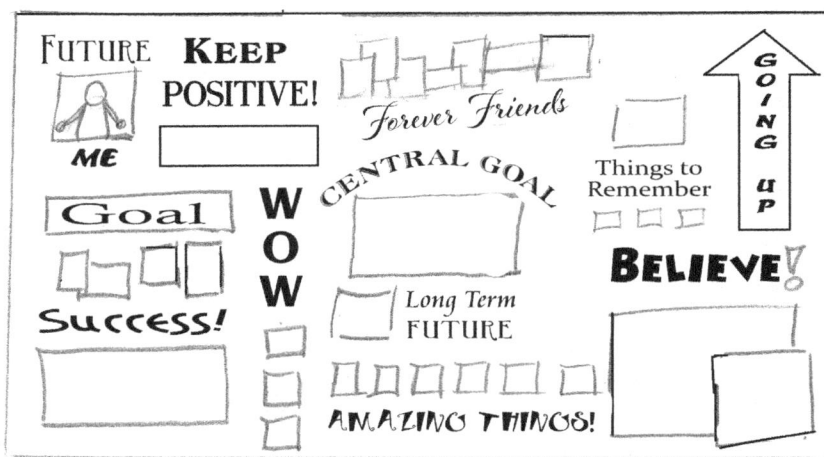

FUTURE **KEEP POSITIVE!**
ME
Forever Friends
CENTRAL GOAL
Things to Remember
GOING UP
Goal
W O W
Long Term FUTURE
BELIEVE!
SUCCESS!
AMAZING THINGS!

Example Vision Board

Presentation

Using any of the writing and/or activities from your **Triumph Journey**, prepare a presentation summarizing what you have accomplished and the goals you have set. Use your **Vision Board** as the centerpiece of this message, walking the audience through **the TRIUMPH you will LIVE** moving forward. This presentation may be done in person as an opportunity to publicly speak about your journey or film a video, edited, and viewed as a masterful production to represent your achievement. If your group has been meeting remotely, this will be the method of choice and is to be created ahead of time. Your **TRIUMPH Speech** should be five to ten minutes long.

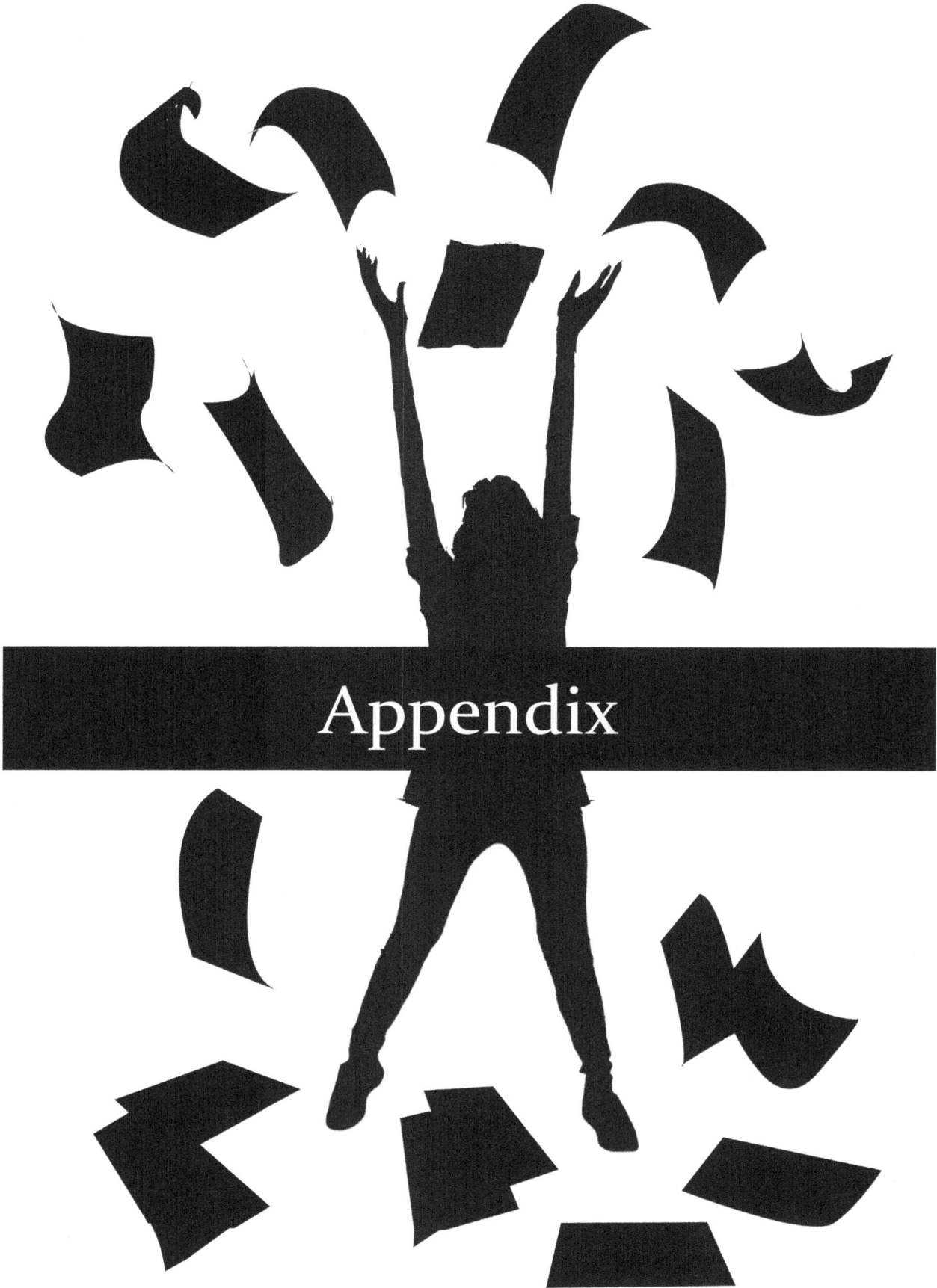

Appendix

The Seven Rules of
Exceptional Writing

Great composition is not the talent of an auspicious few, but a skill which can be developed, practiced and perfected. The following rules of writing can transform your messages from average to extraordinary.

Rule #1- Write Economically

Writing economically is much more than being concise; it is carefully choosing words which pack the greatest meaning into the fewest expressions possible. Economy is one of the most important writing skills you can develop. Many writers have high quality, important ideas, but text-heavy messages often dilute effectiveness as attention spans wane before the point is complete. Consciously or not, people appreciate a concept delivered with brevity and impact. An idea will often appear more ingenious simply because it is written proficiently.

Here is an example-

Bad sentence: You will have much greater success if you avoid being longwinded in your sentences.

Better sentence: Write concise sentences for maximum impact.

Rule #2- Avoid Weak Words

There are certain "casual" or "filler" words which should be avoided in professional or powerful writing. Here are a few examples of weak words: just, lots, get, getting, a lot, really, very, so, pretty much. You should also never use "very" with words that are already superlatives: "very excellent," "very unique," "very wonderful," "very dazzling," "very filthy." The word "awesome" (unless it refers to an erupting volcano or tsunami) should be a crime. It's now a ubiquitous junk word, a verbal virus. Maybe that's just me, but I am often tempted to do a citizens' arrest!

Bad sentence 1: He really gets a lot of attention when he's driving in his very cool car.

Better sentence 1: His flashy red car commands attention when he's behind the wheel.

Bad sentence 2: It's just that you can't be so late without an excuse.

Better sentence 2: Tardiness without an excuse is unacceptable.

Rule #3- Avoid Redundancy

It is easy to utilize the same words over and over without noticing. Repeating words within the same sentence is particularly amateur. Even words as unimportant as "the" can be distracting when overused.

Bad Sentence: The story he told is different than the story she told and the judge was not able to rule based on the disparity between the stories.

Better Sentence: Their stories were vastly different; as a result, the judge made no ruling.

Rule #4- Be Actively Descriptive

Vibrant description is the difference between blah and brilliant composition. Being *actively descriptive* is creating vivid images and using them to do more than illustrate, but also to convey important information.

Passive Description: The petite elderly woman who answered the door appeared weak and frail.

Active Description: The door opened slowly as a petite elderly woman stood, tenderly balancing on her cane.

Rule #5- Use a Thesaurus

A great way to accomplish *Rules 1-4* is to use a Thesaurus, where you can find great words you hadn't considered and which raise the bar on the intelligence quotient of your writing.

Sentence: **Use** a thesaurus to look up the key **words** in your sentences. You may **discover** interesting **options** which carry more **accurate meaning** than the **original** word choice.

Alternate Sentence using a Thesaurus: **Enlist** a thesaurus to look up the key **terms** in your sentences. You may **uncover** interesting **alternatives** which carry more **profound nuances** than the **initial** word choice.

Rule #6- Show, Don't Tell

Wherever possible, **SHOW** your ideas through the use of testimonials, statistics, research, analogies and metaphors. **Evidence** which represents your message will be more convincing than simply stating the point. It also makes your writing more appealing and enjoyable to read.

Example- An analogy showing a female entrepreneur's apprehension:

She felt pain and anxiety as a woman in labor, about to give birth to her long anticipated business endeavor. She was excited to see it fully formed; but also feared for its survival.

Rule #7- Edit, Edit and Edit Again

Powerful, economic, actively descriptive writing with unique phraseology is rarely written the first time. It isn't normal speech pattern, nor is it intuitive for most, and thus many read-throughs may be required. By looking for opportunities to apply these rules when editing, you will create exceptional writing, whatever your topic.

Practice is *the Key!*

When you know the rules of standout composition, you can improve writing ability, no matter your skill level. Until it becomes natural, these skills can be developed through practice. Start by writing a paragraph, perhaps about something related to your story which you would like to use later. Then edit it seven times. Apply the rules one at a time with each edit. For example, the first time you read through the paragraph, check the length of your sentences. Look for expendable words such as *that, the, then, and,* etc., which are unnecessary for the message to be clear. See if you can use stronger words than you have chosen to reduce the amount of text needed to deliver the point. Very long paragraphs can be a good indication that you need to shorten the writing, or at least that the paragraph may need to be broken down into more than one.

Next, read the paragraph looking for weak words. Very often casual words can be removed with little change to the meaning or current sentence structure. Sometimes a sentence will need to be reworked to delete the weak word, but most often they can be removed with little changes required.

In normal speech patterns, overuse of certain words is frequent and finding these issues may be more difficult than you might think. However, your ideas will have more impact and emerge more professional if you reduce the repetition.

In the fourth reading, look for how much detail you have included. If there is very little description, then find the prominent nouns and give them more vibrancy. Instead of passively describing the noun, strive to apply informative significance with adjectives.

The fifth reading will require you to have a Thesaurus (or right click for the synonyms in Microsoft Word... easy!) Underline the main words in your paragraph and look them up. You may be surprised by the variety of suitable options which may create a more interesting or unique message.

In the sixth reading, you will need to stretch creatively or do some research. Define what exactly you are trying to accomplish with the writing; then find evidence to support your position. Include a direct quote, a poem reflecting your ideas or think of an analogy that would shed greater light with its own details.

In the seventh and final reading, do it aloud. This helps to "hear" your message and see if it sounds as well as it reads. It's a great litmus test.

Seven readings may seem tedious, but if you give it a sincere effort, you will be surprised and pleased with the results. As you practice, writing with these rules will become innate, with less work required later. Using these rules of writing will undoubtedly produce exceptional results!

Extra Worksheets

PAST CONFLICT

Describe a past conflict in your life:

Have you overcome this obstacle yet? If so, how? If not, what do you think is holding you back?

What wisdom and strength have you gained from this challenge?

PRESENT CONFLICT

Describe a present conflict in your life:

How do you anticipate overcoming this obstacle?

What wisdom and strength do you believe you will obtain from this challenge?

Things I'm Grateful to have in my Life	Things I'm Grateful NOT to have in my life

Things I am Grateful to have in My Life

Things I'm Grateful to have in my Life	Things I'm Grateful NOT to have in my life

Things I'm Grateful to have in my Life	Things I'm Grateful NOT to have in my life

Things I'm Grateful to have in my Life	Things I'm Grateful NOT to have in my life

Things I'm Grateful to have in my Life	Things I'm Grateful NOT to have in my life

Things I'm Grateful to have in my Life	Things I'm Grateful NOT to have in my life

Mission Statement Prep

Before you write a Mission Statement, it might help to ask yourself these questions:

What are you passionate about?

What difference do you want to make in the world?

How can you use your strengths & talents (or strengths you want to gain) to make that difference?

Now that you've had some self discovery and insight into your future life, contemplate how you can make the most out of your life (in whatever form that takes for you). Use your answers to write your Mission Statement on the following "Mission Statement" worksheet.

Your Personal Mission Statement

S.M.A.R.T.
Short Term Goal

SPECIFIC – What exactly is my goal:

RELEVANT - Fits with my vision: | **Yes** | **No**

MEASURABLE - I will know I have met my goal when:

ACHIEVABLE

Actions I must take to meet my goal:

What **skills** I will use or need to accomplish my goal:

Other help or **things** I need to accomplish my goal. (Ex. To do a painting, you need paints.):

TIME DELINEATED - Due Date: | **Completed "X"**

Long Term Goal

Specific Goal:

Mini-Goal:

Due Date:

Mini-Goal:

Due Date:

Mini-Goal:

Due Date:

X	Actions

X	Actions

X	Actions

Strengths I will use (Can include strengths you wish to gain):

Other things I will Need (Ex. To be a scientist you need a degree):

Anticipated Completion:

Extra Writing Pages

Made in the USA
Las Vegas, NV
25 January 2023